curious about

LACROSSE

BY LISA M. BOLT SIMONS

AMICUS LEARNING

What are you

curious about?

Curious About is published by Amicus Learning, an imprint of Amicus
P.O. Box 227
Mankato, MN 56002
www.amicuspublishing.us

Editor: Grace Cain and Megan Siewert
Series Designer: Kathleen Petelinsek
Book Designer and Photo Researcher: Emily Dietz

Library of Congress Cataloging-in-Publication Data
Names: Simons, Lisa M. Bolt, 1969- author. Title: Curious about lacrosse / by Lisa M. Bolt Simons. Description: Mankato, MN : Amicus Learning, 2025. | Series: Curious about sports | Includes bibliographical references and index. | Audience: Ages 5-9 | Audience: Grades 2-3 | Summary: "Conversational questions and answers share what kids can expect when they join a lacrosse team, including gear to pack, team positions, and how to score points. A Stay Curious! feature models research skills while simple infographics support visual literacy. Includes glossary and index"– Provided by publisher. Identifiers: LCCN 2023043286 (print) | LCCN 2023043287 (ebook) | ISBN 9781645497103 (library binding) | ISBN 9781681529738 (paperback) | ISBN 9781645497165 (ebook) Subjects: LCSH: Lacrosse–Juvenile literature. Classification: LCC GV989.14 .S56 2025 (print) | LCC GV989.14 (ebook) | DDC 796.36/2-dc23/eng/20230929
LC record available at https://lccn.loc.gov/2023043286 LC ebook record available at https://lccn.loc.gov/2023043287

Photo Credits: Alamy/Cal Sport Media, 19; Depositphotos/ProShooter, Cover, 1; Dreamstime/James Boardman, 2, 5, Sports Images, 14–15, 17; Getty Images/Lance King, 6, M. Anthony Nesmith/Icon Sportswire, 20, Ryan Hunt, 21; iStock/browndogstudios, 22, 23, chadster, 2, 10–11, diane555, 17, photosynthesis, 22, 23, Tempura, 3, 13, 18, Yobro10, 6; Shutterstock/enterlinedesign, 13, MarcoVector, 7, Schaafb32, 9, WoodysPhotos, 8

CHAPTER ONE

Is there a lot of running?

Yes! Players need to run fast. They try to get a rubber ball into the other team's goal to score. They also run from **opponents**. Opponents try to knock the ball away.

DID YOU KNOW?

Lacrosse started a long time ago. American Indians first played it. The Iroquois tribe first called it "baggataway."

Your opponent will try to knock the ball away from you.

Wearing goggles and a mouth guard is important for your safety.

What gear do I need to play?

First, you will need protective gear. Boys wear a helmet with a mask. Arm and shoulder pads and gloves are also needed. Girls wear goggles. Both boys and girls wear mouth guards. They carry lacrosse sticks, too.

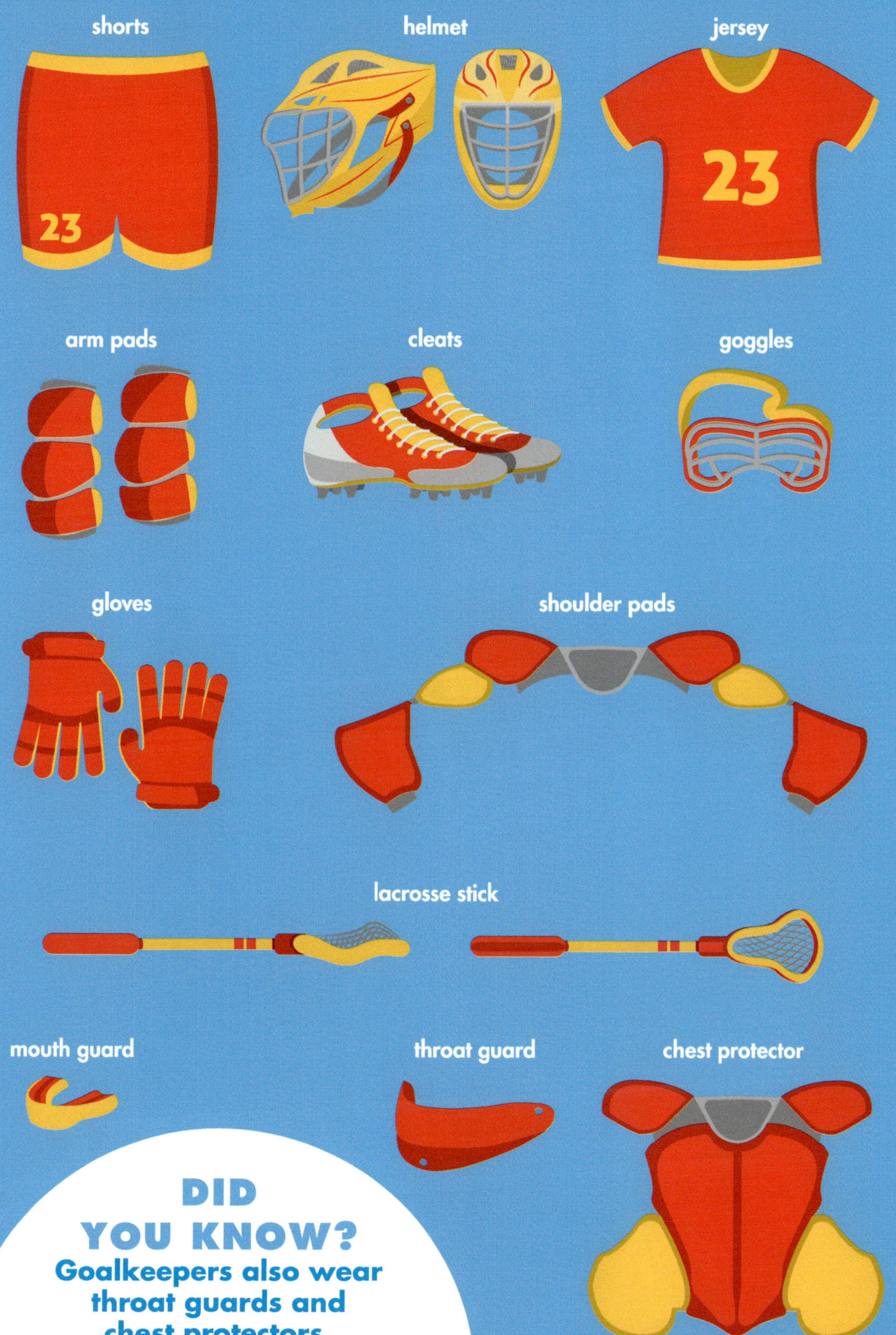

DID YOU KNOW?
Goalkeepers also wear throat guards and chest protectors.

What's the point of the lacrosse stick?

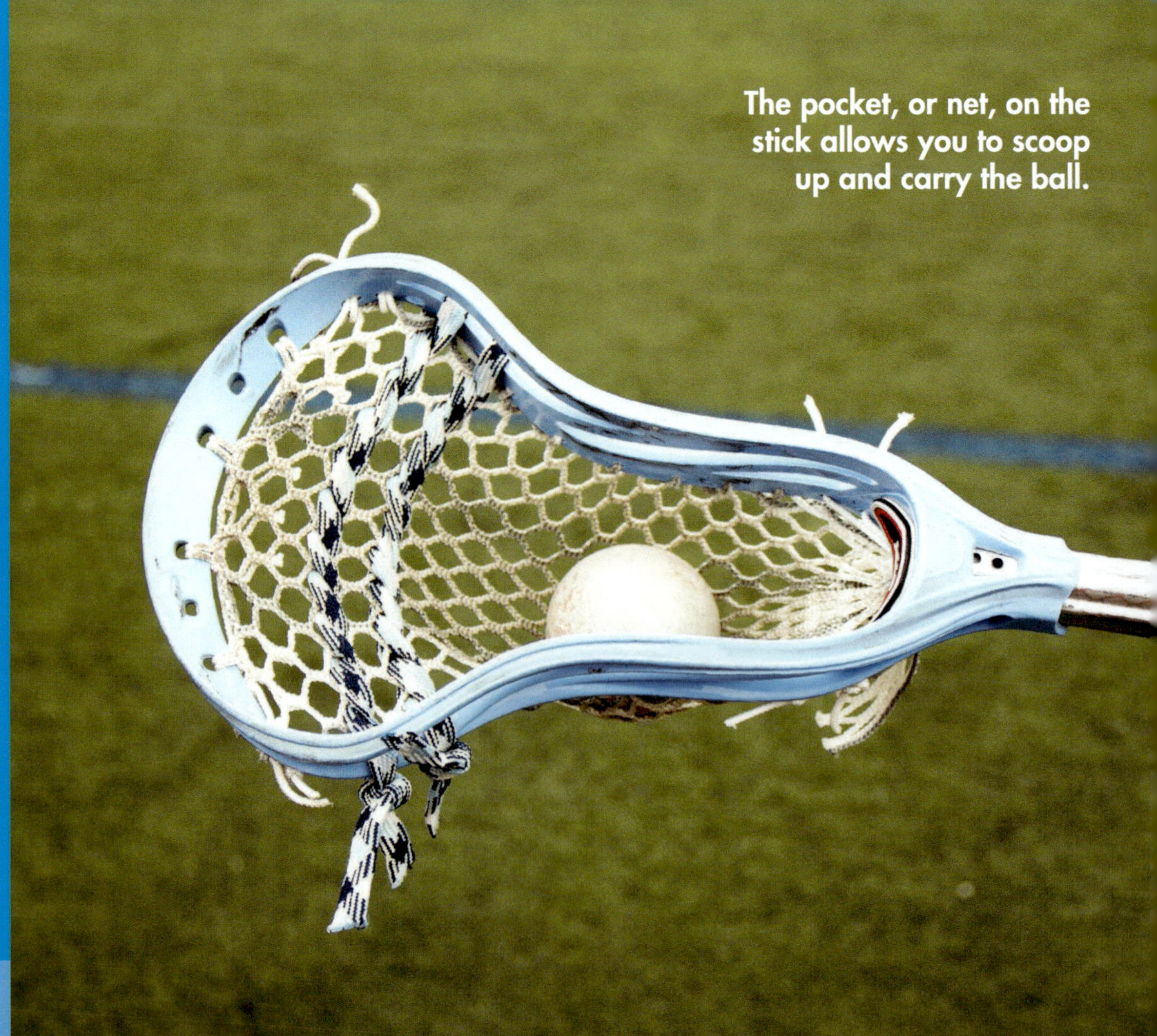

The pocket, or net, on the stick allows you to scoop up and carry the ball.

You use the stick to play. "La crosse" even means "the stick" in French. There is a **pocket** on one end. Players use this to throw and catch. You're not allowed to touch the ball with your hands. Instead, use the stick to scoop it up and shoot.

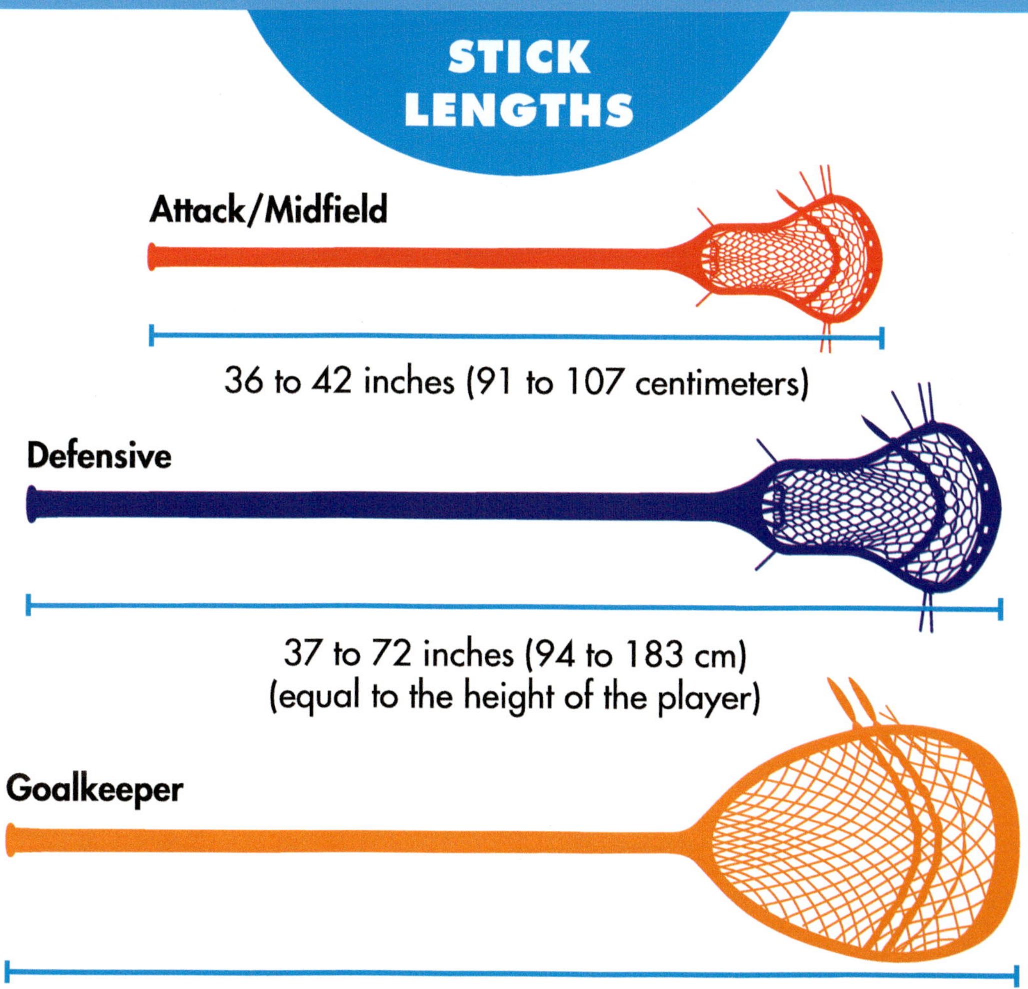

CHAPTER TWO

Which team do I join?

You can join a team of kids your age in your town or city.

Teams are grouped by ages. An 8U team is for kids ages 8 and under. Kids ages 10 and under play on a 10U team, and so on. Many teams are named for the city or by color. For example, you might be on the 8U Springfield team.

How many kids are on my team?

Most boys' teams have 10 players. There are three defenders, three midfielders, three attackers, and a goalkeeper. The goalkeeper and defenders protect the goal. Midfielders play **offense** and **defense**. Attackers score goals. Most girls' teams have an extra attacker and defender.

LACROSSE POSITIONS

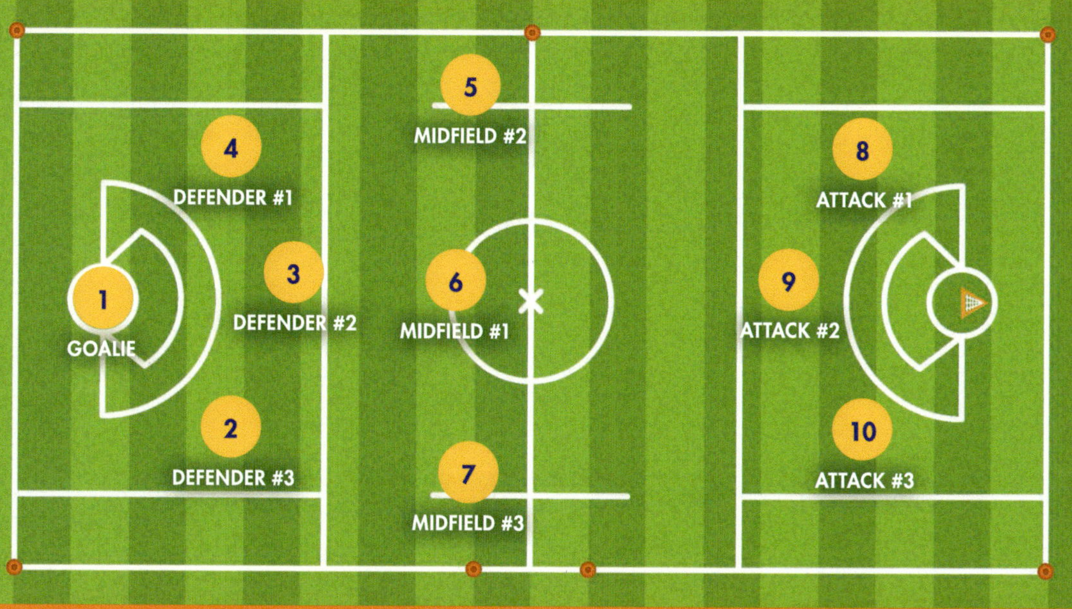

Teamwork is important. Lacrosse players work together to score points and protect the goal.

Who will be my coach?

Someone who loves lacrosse! Often, they played the sport growing up. They may have also played in college, too. Many will be **certified** to coach. Younger teams may have a parent as a coach. Parent coaches are often volunteers.

Your coach will teach you the rules and skills you need to play lacrosse.

How does a lacrosse game start?

A midfielder from each team **faces off**. The referee blows the whistle. The midfielders try to **clamp** the ball on the ground or break it out. The player who wins the ball scoops it up. They may pass it or run toward the opponent's goal to score.

DID YOU KNOW?

Lacrosse is played in more than 75 countries. That number is growing!

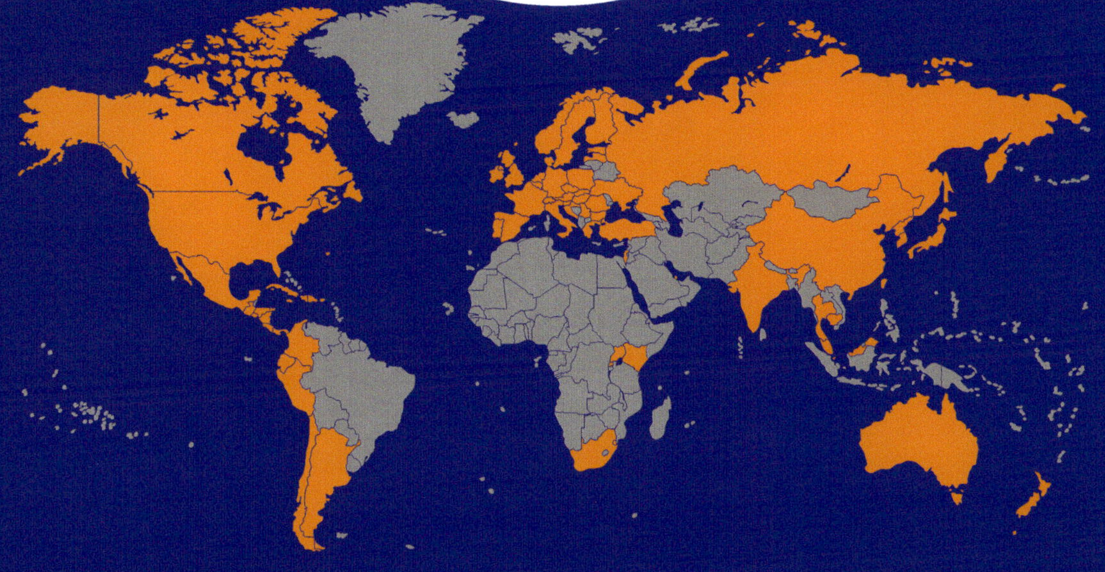

Countries where lacrosse is played

Players face off at the start of every quarter and after every goal.

Spinning your stick while you run helps to keep the ball in the pocket.

What is "cradling"?

It's an important skill. Players **cradle** the ball while running. They spin the stick in half turns while holding it upright. This keeps the ball in the pocket while on the move. The player can protect it from opponents.

DID YOU KNOW?

There are two types of lacrosse. Field lacrosse is played on a field. Box lacrosse is played inside a fence or melted hockey rink.

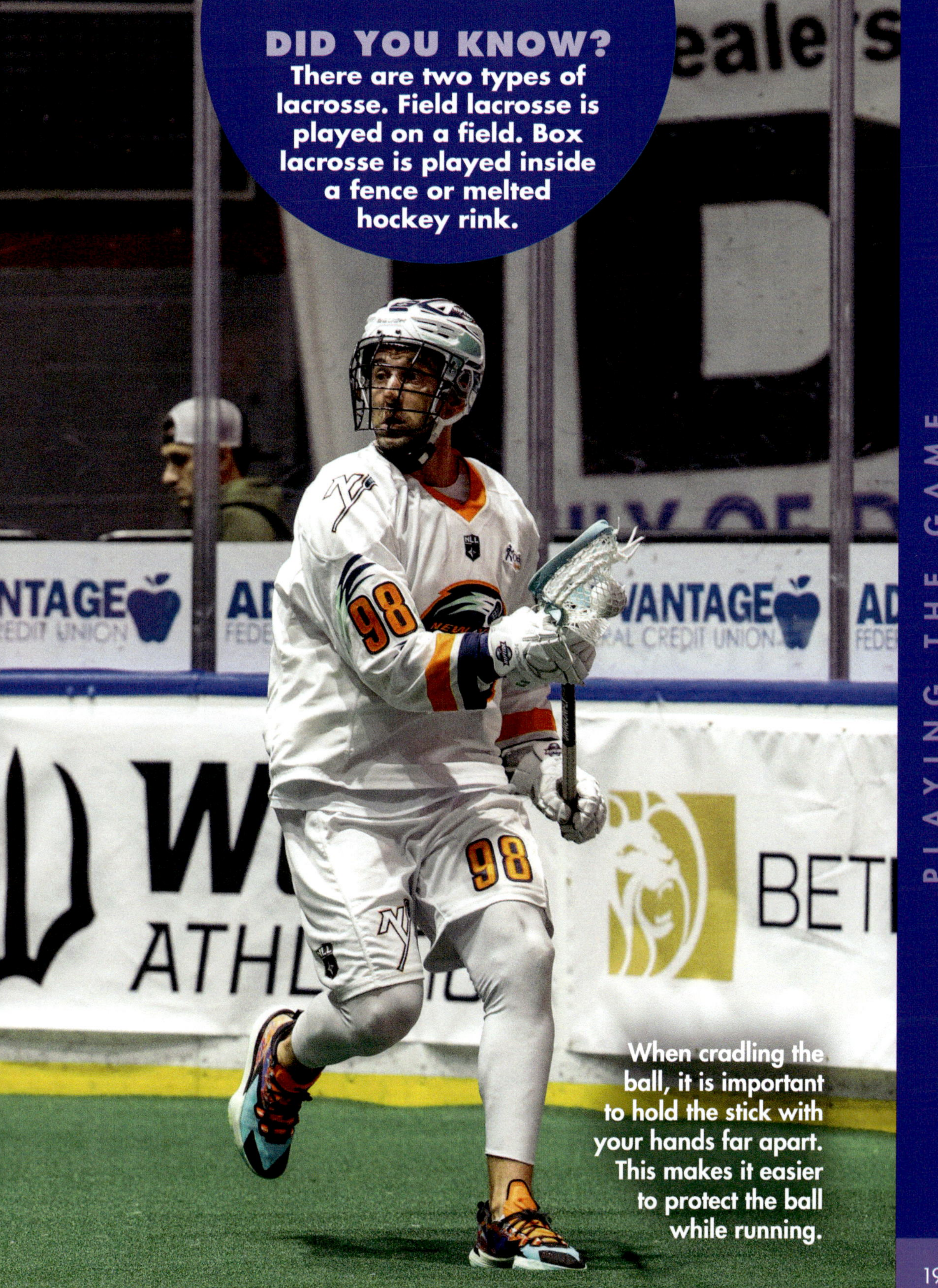

When cradling the ball, it is important to hold the stick with your hands far apart. This makes it easier to protect the ball while running.

How does a team win?

Players move down the field after a face off.

They get the most points! Players scoop, cradle, and pass the ball down the field. Midfielders make sure opponents don't knock the ball away. When an attacker nears the goal, they get ready to shoot. They work around all the defenders. They need just a small opening... Score! One goal equals one point. Keep scoring to win!

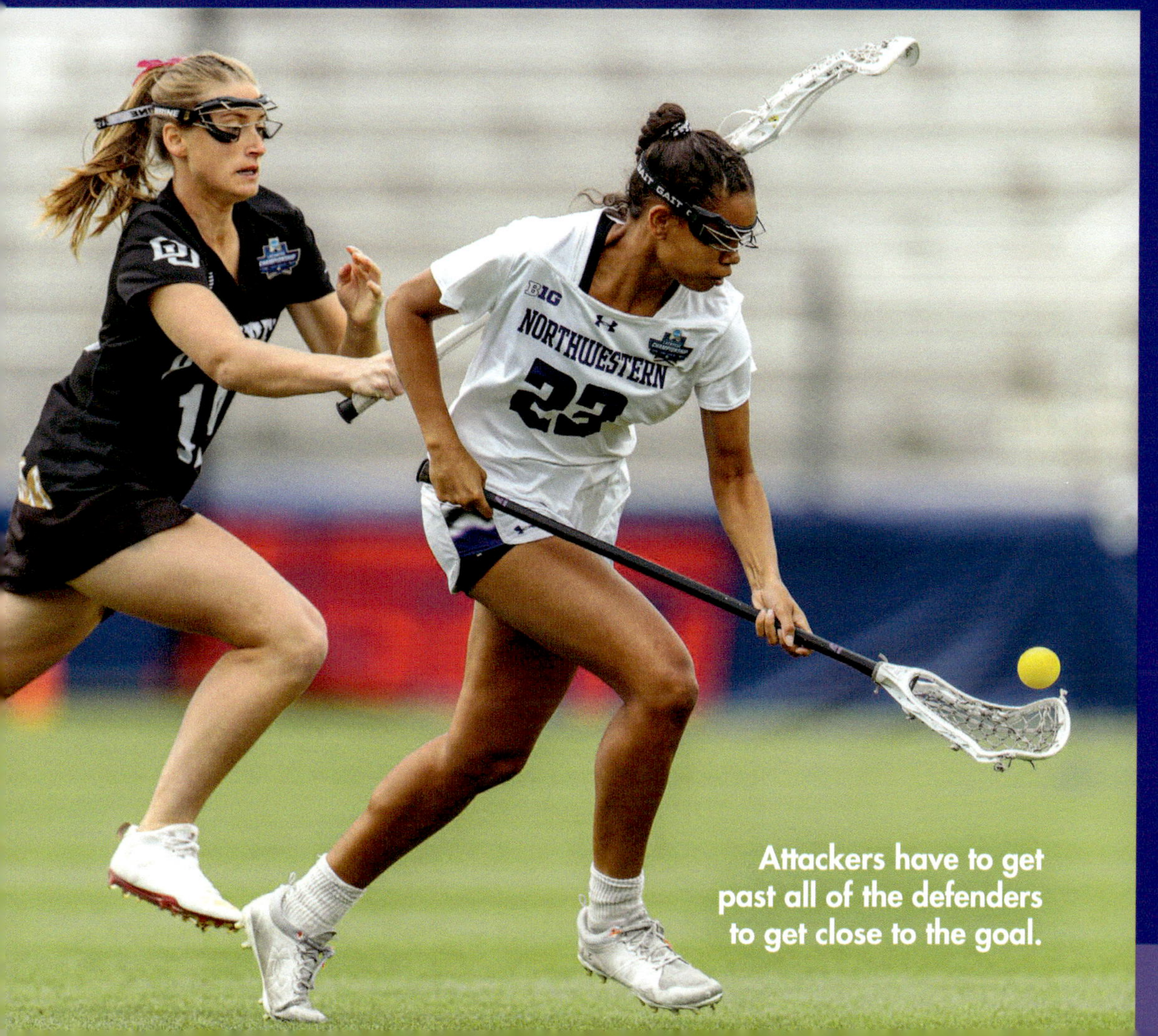

Attackers have to get past all of the defenders to get close to the goal.

STAY CURIOUS!

ASK MORE QUESTIONS

Can I body check other players?

When can I start playing lacrosse?

Try a BIG QUESTION: Is lacrosse a good sport to stay active?

SEARCH FOR ANSWERS

Search the library catalog or the Internet.
A librarian, teacher, or parent can help you.

Using Keywords
Find the looking glass.

Keywords are the most important words in your question.

?

If you want to know about:

- can I check other players, type: LACROSSE CHECKING RULES
- when I can start lacrosse, type: AGE TO START LACROSSE

FIND GOOD SOURCES

Here are some good, safe sources you can use in your research.
Your librarian can help you find more.

Books

Boys' Lacrosse: A Guide for Players and Fans
by Matt Chandler, 2019.

Girls' Lacrosse: A Guide for Players and Fans
by Heather Williams, 2019.

Internet Sites

Lacrosse
https://kids.britannica.com/kids/article/lacrosse/400126
This encyclopedia site covers the rules and equipment for lacrosse, as well as the history of the sport.

USA Youth Lacrosse
https://www.usalacrosse.com/youth-lacrosse
USA Lacrosse is an organization with resources, equipment, and where to play the sport.

Every effort has been made to ensure that these websites are appropriate for children. However, because of the nature of the Internet, it is impossible to guarantee that these sites will remain active indefinitely or that their contents will not be altered.

SHARE AND TAKE ACTION

Go to a track and run laps!
Even if you're not playing yet, you can practice running.

Practice passing and catching a ball with a friend using lacrosse sticks.
See how many times you can go without dropping the ball.

Research great lacrosse players.
What do they do to practice their skills and stay in shape?

GLOSSARY

certified Having met the official requirements that are needed to do a particular type of work.

clamp To hold the ball tightly in the pocket of the stick.

cradle A technique where a player creates a half-circle motion with the stick to carry the ball without dropping it.

defense The players on a team who try to stop the other team from scoring.

face off A physical contest between two opposing players who attempt to gain control of the ball after it is placed on the ground between their sticks.

offense The group of players in control of the ball who try to score points.

opponent A person, team, or group that is competing against another.

pocket The string mesh part of a lacrosse stick used to control the ball.

INDEX

About the Author

Lisa M. Bolt Simons is a writer and retired educator living in Minnesota. She watched lacrosse games at the United States Air Force Academy in Colorado when she was little. She was also a sports mom to her twins, Jeri and Anthony, for more than a decade. She loves doing research to write books for kids.